EYE ON NIXON

EYE ON NIXON

A Photographic Study
of the President and the Man

EDITED BY

Julie Nixon Eisenhower

TEXT BY *William Safire*
Special Assistant to the President

ART DIRECTOR *Byron Schumaker*

W. CLEMENT STONE, PUBLISHER

HAWTHORN BOOKS, INC. / NEW YORK

Royalties from the sale of this book will be donated

to the American National Red Cross

PHOTOGRAPHS BY: President Richard Nixon (page 122): Ollie Atkins,
personal photographer to the President; Jack Kightlinger, Robert
Knudsen, Karl Schumacher, Byron Schumaker, White House photographers; Robert F. Moore, manager of the White House photographic
laboratory.

his is a good year for Chinese proverbs, and the one that applies best to this book is "one picture is worth ten thousand words." *Eye On Nixon* is not a photographic history of the Administration; nor is it an effort to show everything the President does or everywhere he has been. As spoken by the proverb, it is the most concise way of providing insight into the Presidency and the President himself.

I have tried to present a vivid picture of my father as a man—doing his job as President, but more than that, being the kind of man I know him to be—kind, thoughtful, shy, direct, humorous.

He was not a difficult subject. He likes to share the excitement of the Presidency with visitors. That is why, when visitors come to see him, he keeps surprises in the drawers of his Oval Office desk and enjoys handing out the souvenirs. And he will always agree to pose for a group photograph because he wants his visitors to take away a memory. You can see some of the excitement in the picture with the children of the astronauts on Page 98. In the same way, he tries to cooperate with the White House photographers to suggest to the public the moods, triumphs and disappointments of the Presidency.

He does not think of the White House as a "big white jail" or the

Presidency as an "awesome burden," as other Presidents have put it. He enjoys being President because it is the greatest challenge for a man, and because it is the place where one can make things happen.

The pace of the job is in his blood. It shows, I think, in many of the pictures of my father with his advisers and with the leaders of Congress. He has always been an active man, an active listener, and an active participant. The pictures I like best show him absorbed in activity.

The Presidency is a mixture of drama and tediousness, of seriousness and humor, of ceremony and surprise, and that is the flavor I have tried to capture in selecting these photographs. They are arranged schematically to show contrast and association. For example, the photographs of my father dancing (under duress and otherwise), or with world leaders, or just talking on the telephone.

Altogether, the different themes make up the personality of the Presidency—when you concentrate completely on just one part, you miss the point. The same with the personality of my father; he has his moods, like all of us do. The variety of expressions you will see on these pages shows some of the range of those different emotions and reactions.

In this respect, photographs are sometimes the best way to show what a person is really like because they catch fleeting moments. A good example is at the end of the welcoming home ceremony for the Marine division from Vietnam. Probably all of the thousands of viewers at the ceremony did not see my father put his arm around the shoulder of one of the Marines as they walked off the field together. Yet the camera caught that, and this is my father.

It is ironic that I am doing a book of photographs, because the truth is that we have never exactly been a family of photophiles. One of my parents' favorite stories is about the airplane trip the family took from the 1952 Chicago Convention to Denver to see General Eisenhower. It was in the days of the "puddle jumping" airplanes and we made numerous stops en route to Denver. At each stop, the press demanded that we get off the airplane for a family portrait. Finally, at one of the last stops, Tricia—then six years old—took one of the cards reading "occupied" and printed: "There'll be no more pictures." And there weren't. David once asked where my baby pictures were and I had to admit I had none to show him. My father just never took them. He took some pictures of Tricia as a baby, I think, but then lost interest in photographs along those lines—a familiar complaint of the second child in a family.

My mother has always been indifferent about photographs. During the war, when my father wrote asking her to send a picture of herself, she had none available and had to go to a neighborhood photographer—she has never been one to have her picture taken. But in some of the photographs here you see her as the real Patricia Nixon—reaching out to a worker in a Chinese commune, hugging a small child.

So we have few family pictures. My mother said it was always an ordeal to get Tricia and me dressed, and more importantly, in a good mood for a picture. Of course, my father gave her no moral support. Sometimes I am convinced that if my parents were not involved in political life we would not even have the periodic campaign year portraits that are now part of the record.

My father never looks at books of Presidential photographs, just as he does not watch himself on television. He does however, take an avid interest in pictures of us and the things we are doing. For example, if there has been a story about my mother, he shows it to everyone: "Isn't this great?"; "Pat looks so beautiful," and "These are terrific photographs."

I think Tricia and I both place more emphasis on the importance of photographs than our parents do. I guess it is because they are the ones who are so busy and so involved that photographs often seem insignificant. They have so much to accomplish and to endure that they sometimes lose sight of the importance of a pictorial record.

Chinese proverbs notwithstanding, sometimes a mood or a scene can best be captured in words rather than pictures. To sketch these word-pictures, I asked Bill Safire to look over the picture layouts and write what came to mind. Bill has been associated with my father ever since the "kitchen conference" in Moscow in the Fifties; he has an eye for human interest and he has a kind of irreverent approach to things. That is why the running text cannot really be called "captions." They are often word pictures or insights that complement the photographs. The little story about the way my father tried not to give offense to someone he did not want to talk to, on page 41, is a perfect word-snapshot of one facet—and his observation on page 116 about politics not being prose, but being poetry, is an insight into the way he approaches his job that goes beyond photography.

The point is, both in text and in picture selection, this book tries neither to create nor dispel images but rather to capture my father as I have known him. If every photograph showed the President looking marvelous or like a genius, it would be dishonest, and my father would be the first to be embarrassed by it. He looks well most of the time, but the picture of him picking out a necktie with a great, funny look on his face—"the President at his least decisive," as Bill puts it—belongs in here because that is the way he is, too.

He is an optimist. By that I mean he takes an upbeat view of life, thinking more of opportunities than limitations. And his optimism is contagious. Thanks to my father, that positive approach is a part of every member of the family. I recall that time after the defeat of 1960 when he was the one who comforted the rest of us.

The point is, he is convinced there is too much to life that is lost by people who do not see the challenge, who do not take up the opportunities. There definitely is a sense of buoyancy, a feeling of hope, an assurance that "tomorrow will be better" that runs deep in my father's personality. It is this sense of joy of living and confidence that I have tried to capture through photographs. What my father calls "the lift of a driving dream" is good for a person, it is good for a family, and I like to think it is good for a country.

In these pictures, I hope you will get the impression of my father that so many people miss—dignified when he needs to be, but never stuffy; serious about his work, but never taking himself so seriously as to block out warmth and an understanding of the little things.

Ollie Atkins, and the other fine photographers on the White House staff, have opened up their archives for me, and I am grateful to them for their editorial help. Their untiring efforts to assemble photographs over the past three and a half years have made a genuine historical contribution—and, incidentally, have given me the family album I've always wanted.

Julie Nixon Eisenhower

EYE ON NIXON

GETTING ADVICE, NIGHT AND DAY

Feet on the desk, late at night, with
John Ehrlichman and George Shultz,
or head-to-head in the early morning
with John Connally, the President
shapes domestic policy on the basis
of sometimes-conflicting advice from
men he trusts.

He enjoys the political savvy and the
colorful turns of Texas phrase of the
Treasury Secretary: "Mr. President,
I wouldn't trust that feller any
further than I could throw a chimney
by its smoke. . . ."

The President will get advice from a variety of sources—from Julie
Eisenhower, a young woman not reluctant to tell him anything, Counsel
Clark MacGregor (upper right), the chairmen of the Pay Board and
Price Commission, accompanied by Counsellor Donald Rumsfeld, executive
director of the Cost of Living Council.

As can be seen, the President is a clean-desk executive. The silver cigarette
box behind the pens plays "Hail to the Chief" when opened.
It is not often opened.

CONSULTING THE CONGRESS

The President sometimes meets with the bipartisan leaders of Congress
upstairs, in the family quarters of the White House. There, in the Treaty
Room, they sit around a table that once served as the Cabinet table
in the administration of Ulysses S. Grant. This is another indication of
the expansion of the Presidency; Grant's table seats eight comfortably . . .

14

. . . while the current table in the Cabinet Room is designed to seat eighteen. There in the West Wing, protocol is observed—directly to the President's right, in the chair with the brass plaque that says "Secretary of State," sits Senate Majority Leader Mike Mansfield. The meeting with the bipartisan leaders begins when the President enters the Cabinet Room, and the President enters the moment he's told Mike Mansfield is there.

LISTENING

Above is the President at his least decisive, listening to a saleslady's comment on a new tie.

He's a good listener. There are two kinds of listening one does as President: to absorb information and to express concern. On the first, he listens hard—you can feel him chewing over what you're saying, weighing it against what he knows, sifting it for what he can use.

On the second earnest listening, he has a quality that FDR is said to have had: He can focus his attention on one person and make that person feel he or she is the only one who concerns the President of the United States.

GIVING ORDERS

The President frequently accompanies an order with a gesture of his left hand. "This is what I've decided" or "Here's what we'll do" is spoken in a low tone, usually directed to H. R. Haldeman, Henry Kissinger, George Shultz or (below) John Ehrlichman. Once in a while, when he anticipates resistance down the line, he will add: "Don't let the bureaucracy fuzz it up. That's an order."

"I DO SOLEMNLY SWEAR . . ."

Richard Nixon was sworn in as 37th President of the
United States by a fellow Californian, Chief Justice
Earl Warren; at left, he takes another oath, which
makes him a voter in the State of California.

He lives in the White House; he has a house in Florida
and a retreat in the mountains of Maryland; but
California is "home."

CABINET MEETING

Ever notice the way the President enters
a room? He never pokes his head in,
or saunters in casually, or enters
tentatively—on the contrary, he makes
an entrance, sweeping in or striding
in authoritatively, automatically
taking charge.

That's deliberate; making an entrance
is a part of making a strong impression
and answering a need for leadership.
If you happen to be the aide opening the
door of a meeting room at Camp David
(left), a rally auditorium, the
Cabinet Room (above) or the
Presidential aircraft—pull it open and
get out of the way.

The Cabinet Room is also a place for briefing; outside is the Rose Garden,
which is a tulip garden in the spring and a chrysanthemum garden
in the fall. The President likes to conduct an occasional private session
out there; in the picture at left, he chats with Secretary of State Rogers and
UN Ambassador Bush.

HOST

The White House is the Executive
Mansion and the President's house—
a museum, an office and a home on
a single site. Entertaining at home is
an important part of the Presidency,
and Nixon enjoys it—from a swinging
dinner honoring Duke Ellington
to a formal state occasion. At left, the
welcoming of a distinguished visitor
as seen from the Treaty Room
upstairs in the Residence; below, a
black tie state dinner. All is not pomp
and circumstance, however; part of
the Nixon imprint on the White
House is . . .

. . . the Sunday morning church services—here, a
Christmas service with the families of the
Administration, White House staff and other friends
in attendance. On the receiving line afterward, a
flustered visitor invariably says, "It's a President,
Mr. Pleasure."

The White House can be turned into
an art gallery with ease—Andrew Wyeth,
the great American painter, was
given a reception and his works were
shown for several weeks afterward.
As the reception ended, the President
steered a guest over to a brooding
seascape: "That's the one I like best.
Wish we could keep it."

Presidents think on exalted levels. When the President of Nicaragua sent him a box of cigars, the President wondered aloud, "Who do I know who smokes cigars?" His aides came up with a few pedestrian ideas, then the President snapped his fingers and said, "I know—Tito."

President Tito did come to repay a visit in October of 1971; he was not only offered cigars but a close look at one of the scenic wonders of the White House—the Presidential Seal set into the ceiling of the Oval Office. It's not all that exciting to observe, but no visit to the center of power is complete without a craning of necks to look at the seal, pictured at left.

At the opening of the Eisenhower Theater at the Kennedy Center for the Performing Arts.

Here are contrasting aspects of the President as host: left, informally welcoming some photographers to his San Clemente, California, home and below, at one of the jam-packed Inaugural Balls.

THE WORD "POLITICIAN"

Sometimes a man says a lot about himself when he talks about another man. Working on the eulogy to Senate Minority Leader Everett Dirksen, the President said, "Ev was a politician and proud of it—he never shied away from that word. I want to show how he gave luster to the word 'politician.'"

This is how the President defined the term at the memorial services:

"A politician knows that more important than the bill, that is proposed is the law that is passed.

"A politician knows that his friends are not always his allies and that his adversaries are not his enemies.

"A politician knows how to make the process of democracy work, and loves the intricate workings of the democratic system.

"A politician knows not only how to count votes, but how to make his vote count.

"A politician knows that his words are his weapons, but that his word is his bond.

"A politician knows that only if he leaves room for discussion and room for concession can he gain room for maneuver.

"A politician knows that the best way to be a winner is to make the other side feel it does not have to be a loser.

"And a politician—in the Dirksen tradition—knows both the name of the game and the rules of the game, and he seeks his ends through the time-honored democratic means."

36

THINKING

A supporter of William Jennings Bryan once boasted that his candidate had made 19 speeches in a single day, to which an opponent replied: "When does he think?"

The President builds thinking time into his calendar. Wednesdays, for example, are kept relatively clear of appointments to allow time to ponder, to read and to ask a few searching questions.

He can be interrupted. Oddly, you are not expected to knock on the door when entering the President's office, presumably on the theory that you would not be there if you should not be. But when he's chewing things over, it's not a good idea to go in with something trivial.

"THE PRESIDENT IS CALLING YOU"

In an age when an unlisted telephone number is both a status symbol and a defense against cranks, it is comforting to note that the phone number of the President of the United States is listed in the District of Columbia telephone directory—456-1414, under "White House."

But not many people pick up the phone to call the President. After a major speech the White House switchboard gets inundated with calls, and the President sometimes chews over reactions with callers he knows until the early morning. In the normal course of a day, he will receive less than a half-dozen calls from outside the official family.

Richard Nixon uses the telephone to get a piece of information, to thank someone, to cheer up a shut-in, or to give an order—rarely to chat. If he wants to chew the fat with someone, he invites him over.

Since the people with normal "access to the President" don't abuse the opportunity to get through to him on the phone, he is inclined to take a call. One night, working on a speech on foreign affairs in his private office in the Executive Office Building (across the street from the White House), the phone rang and he picked it up. He listened to a question and then took about ten minutes to explain the current state of Latin American relations. An aide took notes, figuring it might fit in the speech, and after the President hung up, asked who he had been speaking to—Secretary Rogers or Henry Kissinger?

"That was Julie," the President said. "She's being interviewed in the morning for a USIA broadcast to Brazil." He then picked up the speech where he had left off.

Sometimes, of course, he'll duck a call, but he doesn't like to be rude. An aide once asked him if he wanted to talk with so-and-so; the President shook his head, groped for an excuse, and suggested: "Tell him you can't find me."

SPEAKING

He wants his communications "mix" to have a lot of different ingredients. At left, television cameras in the Oval Office cover a phone call to the first men to walk on the moon; below, he addresses the AFL-CIO convention in Miami, Florida; at right, in the library, he chats with four network correspondents in a year-end wrap-up.

Nothing turns the President on,
however, like the stimulus of a live
audience and the feeling of getting out
into the country. You can see it on
his face here in Phoenix, Arizona, and,
overleaf, you can feel the intimacy
of a crowd of students at University of
Nebraska. . . .

PERFECTLY CLEAR

After the fourth or fifth time he used
"Let me make one thing perfectly clear" at
news conferences like the regional briefing in
Los Angeles pictured here, the phrase
became part of Nixon lore and was parodied,
like Lyndon Johnson's "continya" and
John Kennedy's "vigah." Subsequently, the
President caught himself after the "Let me"
and substituted "be quite blunt" or
"speak very frankly about this."

But when a questioner wanted to clarify a
query in a press conference and started to
say, "I want to make sure I'm being . . . ,"
the President interrupted him to help out:
"Perfectly clear." It got a laugh, and the
President made the point that he was aware of,
but not uptight about, his speaking habits.

FAMILY ALBUM

48

FATHER OF THE BRIDE
At Tricia's shower, gifts, admired here by Mamie Eisenhower, ranged from a feather boa to a gold telephone from Martha Mitchell. Controversy swirled around the wedding cake when a reporter tried the recipe and decreed that it had to be a flop. (It turned out fine.)

Though the day was overcast, both father and daughter were determined to hold the ceremony outdoors in the Rose Garden. As Julie describes it, the tension built toward the time of the ceremony; the President paced around in the upstairs living room, looking out the window down at the Rose Garden and glowering back at the sky. Then he said, "Where are the chairs? Why aren't those chairs out there?" and barked orders into the phone.

The chairs were there, the rain held
back, and with faces serenely composed,
father and daughter made their
appearance.

DANCING

These may be the only two pictures around of President Nixon dancing— at Tricia's wedding and during his trip to Romania.

His wife and daughters insist that he is a perfectly capable dancer, but as a dancer, he's a good President.

ABOARD *THE SPIRIT OF '76*

The Presidential aircraft have been called
*The Sacred Cow, The Columbine,
Air Force One,* and now *The Spirit of '76,*
and each President uses his plane
more than the last.

During the interregnum, President
Lyndon Johnson made the plane
available to the President-elect for a
trip to Key Biscayne. Richard Nixon sat
in the easy chair in the President's
flying office for the first time, called a
few aides in, and pushed a button. The
coffee table elevated itself into a
conference table. He swiveled around,
smiled, took a deep breath, and
observed: "It beats losing."

QUICK GETAWAY

The President's helicopter, *Marine One,* may be a noisy place for a conference, but it makes all the difference in travel time. Below, flying into Chicago.

WORLD LEADERS

British Prime Minister Edward Heath, arriving in good weather, gets the full treatment for a visiting head of government at the White House. Emperor Hirohito of Japan, passing through Alaska, gets head-of-state honors as he stands on U.S. soil for the first time. At all these occasions, the President is ready with "appropriate remarks"—never read from a script but always carefully thought out beforehand.

Some people think Soviet Foreign Minister Andrei
Gromyko and President Nixon are look-alikes. Gromyko
is the one on the left, probably.

On a trip to Paris, the President was given a detailed schedule by the State Department that included a small error: "President Nixon will speak for ten minutes, following which his remarks will be translated into English." He kidded the Embassy staff: "I knew I had trouble communicating, but I didn't realize it was that bad. . . ."

With Premier Trudeau of Canada

With President de Gaulle of France

With President Thieu of South Vietnam on Midway Island

With Chancellor Willy Brandt of West Germany in the Green Room of the White House

In Rome, following an audience with the Pope, the President met with a group of American priests and told them of an odd feeling he sometimes had—of wakening with a feeling that there was something important that he had to tell the President, an instant before remembering that he was the President.

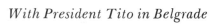
With President Tito in Belgrade

With General Franco in Madrid

PREPARING FOR THE SUMMITS

Before his "journeys for peace" to Peking and Moscow, the President met with Western leaders. Left, with Prime Minister Sato in San Clemente; below, with Prime Minister Heath in Bermuda; right, with Chancellor Brandt in Florida; below right, with President Pompidou in the Azores.

At the Bermuda Conference, aboard
H.M.S. *Glamorgan* for the official dinner,
the President noted the motto of the
Welsh-named ship: "Aim for the
Highest." Since it was the week after
some tough negotiating on currency
alignments, he added. "That just
happens to be the motto of the Secretary
of the Treasury, also."

With Chou En-lai in Peking—
the opening handshake of "the week
that changed the world."

During most of the talks, both principals used a normal conversational tone; at crucial moments, however, when each leader wanted to make an important point, he did the opposite from what one might expect: He spoke especially quietly, since each knew the other would be more impressed with restraint than bombast.

With Chairman Mao

In the afterdinner toasts, each word was weighed.

In the photo at left, there is no telling what was going through the President's mind as he examined the morsel at the end of his chopsticks.

At right, Mrs. Nixon visits a panda; below, she reaches across a trellis in the greenhouse of the Evergreen People's Commune, outside Peking, to greet a commune worker.

Sightseeing in China, a lifelong dream of the President's, and an important part of an official visit. The symbol of Republicanism, at left, provided some fun, but the symbolism of the Great Wall, at right, did not go unmentioned in major world capitals.

WORKING THE FENCE

Breaking protocol and crossing over to a crowd of well-wishers to shake hands is called "working the fence" in political lingo, and the President is an unabashed practitioner of the art.

Let's face it—some of the "impromptu" stops along a motorcade route are meticulously scouted by advance men. But others are not, and Secret Service men roll up their eyes and follow along when the President spots a group of people he wants to greet, barks "Stop here" and plunges into the crowd.

On a sentimental journey (above) to his Quaker ancestors' home in Timahoe, Ireland, some friendly oglers on horseback galloped alongside the motorcade. The President stopped the car and despite the lack of a fence, "worked the fence."

The first time we spotted a "Welcome Mr. Peace" sign
was in Columbus, Ohio, in October 1970.

There is always the suspicion that hand-lettered signs along the campaign trail are secretly mass-produced in some political backroom. But what politician, amateur or professional, would have the daring and imagination to misspell the President's name? It had to be for real.

"PHOTO OPPORTUNITY"

Presidents and councilmen share the same responsibility to pose for staged publicity pictures. These are "pseudo-events," from the symbolism of planting a tree in India to tugging on a rope at Libby Dam in Montana to release a yard of concrete for the dam. The President not only goes along with this game but takes an active hand in the making of the picture the photographers want: "Ready, Mike? All together now—pull!"

COMMANDER IN CHIEF

All Commanders-in-Chief have a special affinity for the men in the armed forces, and Nixon, a former Navy lieutenant, is no exception. Mingling with troops in Vietnam (left) or welcoming home the First Marine Division from Vietnam at Camp Pendleton, California, the President is both moved and moving. The arm around the GI's shoulder, walking back after the ceremony, was a natural impulse from a man not given to public displays of affection, and the photographer caught a poignant moment.

Manolo Sanchez, who has been Richard Nixon's valet, coffee-getter and utility infielder since 1962, is the one who is "there" at all hours. Soon after the Kent State tragedy, during a night when the President found sleep difficult, he took Manolo to the Lincoln Memorial and then to the Capitol in the hours before dawn. A cleaning woman let them into the House of Representatives, where the President applauded from the back when Manolo slipped into the Speaker's chair.

The two men have worked out a unique form of communication, based on English used only in the present tense, with a mutual Spanish accent: "We go soon." "We go now?" "We go."

Above, the guest register on an historic weekend—
August 13–15, 1971, when the New Economic Policy
was set in place. The President worked all night
on his speech freezing prices and ending the
convertibility of the dollar into gold, and a Navy
chief was startled to see the President stroll
out into the early dawn.

The President handed him some dictaphone tapes
and asked him to take them over to Rose Mary
Woods's cabin for typing. As the chief left, the
President took a few deep breaths of the morning air,
yawned and went back inside for a morning's
sleep. It's a good place for creative work.

And it's a fine place for a thoughtful stroll—right,
on a crisp winter afternoon with British
Prime Minister Heath.

CAMP DAVID

President Franklin Roosevelt called it "Shangri-la" after the Himalayan
hideaway in James Hilton's *Lost Horizon*; Dwight Eisenhower renamed
it Camp David; in the Kennedy and Johnson years, it was sometimes called
"Camp Three"; now it is Camp David again and active as it has
never been before.

The David in the name is, of course, David Eisenhower, married to the
President's younger daughter, Julie (who selected the pictures in
this book). The guest register in Aspen, the President's cabin, has the name
"David" scrawled in block letters in the early pages and the same name
written as an adult more recently.

WITH YOUNG PEOPLE

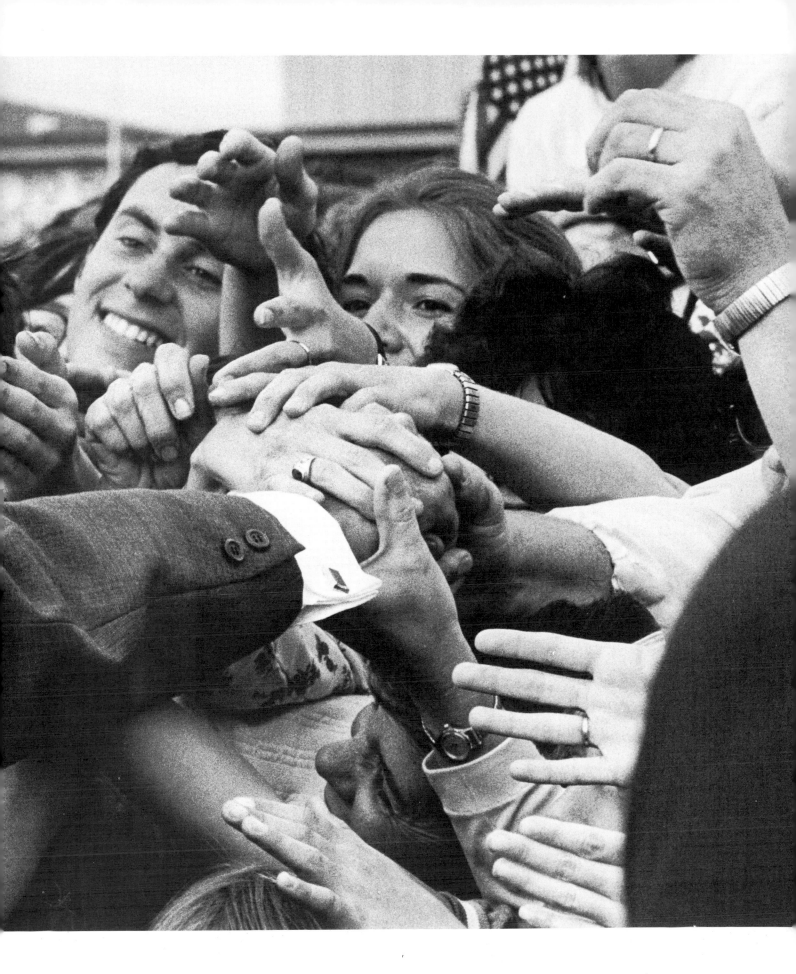

In the imposing Presidential desk in the Oval Office, there are drawers
that could qualify as the local drop for a souvenir manufacturer—containing
pens, pins, golf balls, paperweights, tie clasps, you-name-'em-we've-got-'em.

Kids, their eyes wide in wonderment, get the biggest kick out of the souvenir
ceremony—the desk seems to turn into a candy-store cornucopia.

President to a six-year-old boy: "I'd like to give you cuff links, but you
don't wear cuff links." Quick comeback: "I sure will now!"

THE FIRST LADY

She works hard, and she's good to work with.

An example: When Nixon was a New York lawyer, she would pitch in at the office handling the "overload"— the calls and correspondence that never stopped coming from political friends. To preserve the office atmosphere, she used her maiden name: Miss Ryan.

Occasionally, a caller wanted to go over the head of the girl who answered the phone. This usually came in the form of "Look, Miss Ryan, you're very nice and helpful, but I want to make sure this goes to somebody close to Mr. Nixon." Without batting an eye, she would assure the caller that she would see to it that the message reached somebody close to Mr. Nixon.

Kids have a way of sensing genuine
warmth. She gets hugged good and hard.

The picture that is *not* here is of Mrs. Nixon welcoming Jacqueline
Kennedy Onassis and her children to the White House to a private dinner.
That is because, at Mrs. Nixon's direction, no picture was taken.
What might have been a painful occasion was turned into one of
graciousness, warmth, privacy and great good taste by a First Lady who
not only knows how to treat former First Ladies but is also a woman who
understands what is felt in other people's hearts.

Visits hospital in Thailand

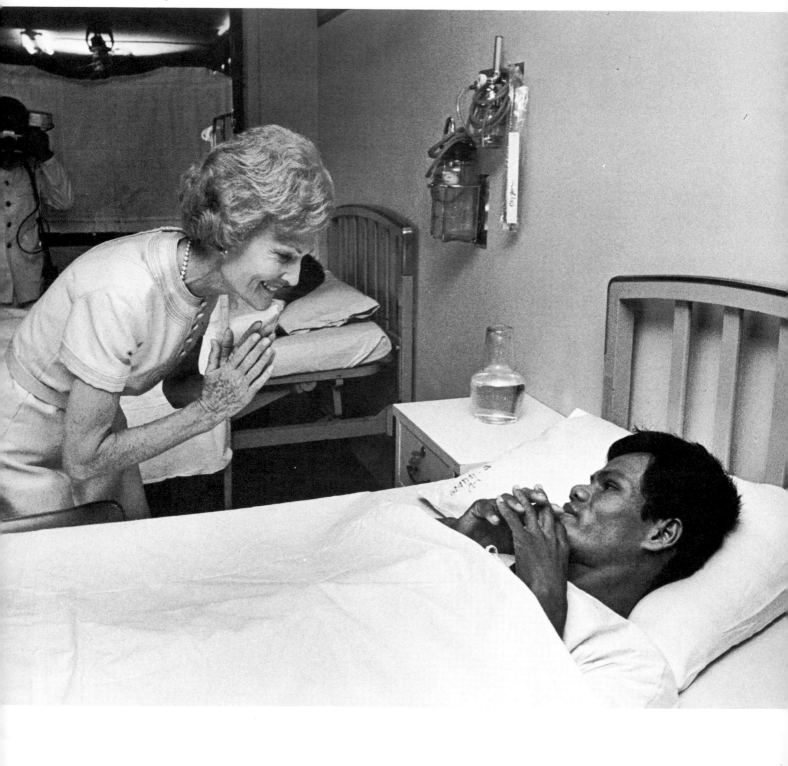

The visit to Africa—a goodwill tour
all her own.

The President likes to be on the water and in the water; fresh air and salt spray do something for him, and accessibility to a beach (California, Florida, the Bahamas) has always been a part of his life.

In a Key Biscayne beach house one day in 1965, talking politics with Bebe Rebozo and another friend, Nixon announced he was going to take a dip and went outside. Bebe fidgeted a couple of minutes, then murmured, "He shouldn't be in the ocean by himself," and followed along. These days, there are Secret Service men for that.

DOGS

Before she married Dick Nixon, Pat Ryan would occasionally look after his dog, an Irish setter named King. To say thanks, he bought her a little china statuette of a setter; that little china dog, on loan from Mrs. Nixon, now is one of the few mementos on his desk in the Executive Office Building.

When an Irish setter joined the Nixon family in the White House (along with a poodle and a Yorkshire terrier that came with them from New York), the inclination was to call him King, after that first dog. That formal name was hardly appropriate for a dog belonging to the President of a democratic country, however, and the Nixons cast about for another name. Jessamyn West, author of *Friendly Persuasion* and the President's cousin, came up with Timahoe, after the village in County Kildare, Ireland, home of the President's forebears. The official name, then, is King Timahoe; Manolo Sanchez sometimes calls him Timmy, but the family calls him King.

The President and the First Lady do not see eye to eye about the right of large dogs to jump up on and sprawl all over furniture. Since this has not been resolved between them, King Timahoe has come up with a compromise: He sprawls on a sofa, looking guilty.

In the EOB office

With Emperor Haile Selassie

At San Clemente

SPORTS

With Redskins coach George Allen and quarterback Bill Kilmer, the President believes "the future is now," and his enthusiasm for the team rings true. (At the Azores Conference with President Pompidou, Bill Rogers groggily received a call from President Nixon at 2 A.M., to hear "I knew you'd still be up, Bill, and you'd want to know the score at half time. . . .")

The President is a spectator. His golf game is not very good, and he wistfully recalls the days when he never made it off the bench at Whittier College. But there are bowling alleys at Camp David and in the Executive Office Building, and his game is improving.

One afternoon, he entered a room and proudly announced he'd scored 130. Henry Kissinger said he was glad to hear the President enjoyed golf, and the President growled, "I was bowling, Henry."

WRITING

"Keep it short," he tells his writers.
"When you have a lot to say, you don't
have to say a lot."

The trouble with writing speeches for
Nixon is that Nixon likes to write
speeches for himself. He spends more
time writing than any President since
Woodrow Wilson.

He works alone, usually in the EOB
office or the Lincoln Sitting Room in the
White House. It starts in ink on the
yellow pad as rough notes; he then
dictates a draft from these notes into a
recorder, which Secretary Rose Mary
Woods types up. Then a writer will get a
crack at it. But only one writer—Nixon
will not work on a speech with a
committee. (FDR was different; Robert
E. Sherwood, Samuel Rosenman and
Harry Hopkins would sit around the end
of the Cabinet table to craft a speech.)

The style is spare. The presentation is organized, leading to an orderly conclusion. Few flights of oratory, few explanations in detail, no apologies. On the peroration, however—the exhortation at the end of a speech—he will loosen up to find that "lift of a driving dream." The ending he likes most centers on an anecdote or historical parallel, like John Brown on his way to the gallows, musing, "This is a beautiful country."

He has a writer's taste for metaphor. Talking politics one night, an aide made some point about a logical next development. "No, no," he said, "you're treating politics like prose. Politics isn't prose; politics is poetry."

SIGNING

Above, he signs the bill that enables 18-year-olds to vote.

The most dramatic signing ceremony was probably his first veto—which he did live on television, the signature punctuating the end of his speech. Just before Nixon went on the air, a legal expert whispered, "He's got the bill and the veto message in front of him. If he signs the wrong one, that bill becomes a law." The President was aware of the pitfall; when the moment came, he carefully set the bill aside and signed the veto, and we all relaxed.

Photographing the President

By OLLIE ATKINS, *Personal Photographer to President Nixon*

Can you imagine the President of the United States ordering a photographer to "make one more"?

One time when President Nixon suddenly decided I'd better try "one more" was in Hangchow, China, in a courtyard of what we think was Chairman Mao's summer home. I was making a group picture in the good old Chinese style of the President with all the American correspondents traveling with him on the famous China trip. It was rather damp and chilly, and I didn't waste any time clicking off three or four frames of the group. But President Nixon wanted to be very, very certain I had not goofed and told me to "take one more, Ollie."

Of course, the above is all done in good humor. I find the President very easy to photograph. There are no rules about photographing him this way or that, and I make a determined effort to do my work speedily so the necessary photography is as painless as possible.

Some of the very best photographs of him were done when I could just slip into his office, or the room where he was working, and quietly make two or three exposures and move out without ever saying a word.

My job is to produce an historic, photographic documentation of the administration of President Nixon. Many of these photographs can be used for current publication. I work under the direction of Ronald Ziegler, Press Secretary to the President, with the press photographers in general and the "pool" when transport and space necessarily limit the number of press in the immediate presence of the President.

President Nixon is very "savvy" about the requirements of both the writing and the photographic press. His long experience in the House of Representatives, in the Senate and as Vice President has taught him that press photographers are professionals. He is aware of their technical needs. Certainly, photographs cannot be made without light—usually blinding floodlights.

He understands that press cameramen are the eyes of the public and that
their pictorial reports inform the people of important events involving
the Presidency. Still, he doesn't ham it up or repeat things time after time
for the benefit of the cameras.

One of President Nixon's traits most appreciated by the press photographers
is his accurate scheduling. Thing happen pretty much on time. Also,
little things that go wrong from time to time do not upset him.

For instance, recently at Libby Dam, Montana, President Nixon and
Senator Mansfield were to pull a rope dumping a large bucket of concrete
into the dam structure. The workmen had prepared the concrete too far in
advance and it had set, so when the rope was pulled, the concrete
wouldn't flow. The President and Senator Mansfield pulled furiously;
still the stubborn concrete would not bulge. Workmen shook up the
mixture with jackhammers, and the next time they pulled, the concrete
poured forth. Everyone got fine pictures (see page 85), and the President
was not the least concerned that the ceremony was slightly fouled up.

Of course, there are problems. One of the toughest is being in the right
place on time when the President is moving from point to point. Reasonable
security is a requirement. Once in Birmingham, Alabama, I was trying
to take the two wire-service photographers to a rooftop vantage point for
an overall crowd scene when a local policeman stopped me. He was on
duty guarding the entrance, and he had orders that "nobody was permitted
there." I showed him my White House credentials, but orders were *orders*.
Luckily, I spotted another law officer who happened to be an old
classmate of mine in college, and he slipped me to the roof
by another route.

I think the public deserves a truthful impression of what the President
really is and not some romantic and preconceived notion of what some
photographer or art director thinks he ought to be. When one spends
considerable time around the President, a special impression comes
through which is that Richard Nixon is a man with "peace at the center."
I find no trouble in photographing him as such.

The Nixons know this strip of beach near their home in San Clemente.
On those bluffs overlooking the sea, he proposed to her thirty years ago, so
there is a sentimental feeling attached to it. And it's one of the
few places they can take a long walk alone.

Picture Index

PRODUCTION NOTES

The text type, 11 point Baskerville, was set by Lino-Tech, Inc., New York, New York.

Color separations were made by Bob Vari, Long Island City, New York, and Seidel, Farris, Clark, Inc., Toledo, Ohio.

The text paper is Westvaco's Sterling Matte, White, 80 lb.

The printing and binding was done by web offset by Kingsport Press, Kingsport, Tennessee.

Production planning was done by Samuel J. Green and Stanley S. Drate.

Typography by Stanley S. Drate.